# WHO IS TOUGHER?

## NAVY SEALs VS. ARMY RANGERS

RANGER

# by Jerry Pallotta
# Scholastic Inc.

Photos ©: 123RF: 28, 29 map (experimental), 1 Ranger silhouette (zabelin); Altama Boots: 2 right; Bill Nicholson: 11 bottom, 16 folder, 16 words throughout, 17 right helicopter, 26, 27 t-shirt designs; Clker.com/Mohamed Ibrahim: 1 SEAL silhouette; Department of Defense/Senior Airman Jason Epley, U.S. Air Force: 25 bottom; DVIDS: 8 top (Donna Miles), 10 top (Kyle Gahlau), 14 bottom (Petty Officer 2nd Class Anthony Harding), 12 center (Petty Officer 3rd Class Adam Henderson), 23 (Sgt. Brian Kohl), 3 top (U.S. Army photo by Spc. Coty Kuhn); Freeimages/David Ritter: cover sign background; Getty Images/ Mitch Frazier/U.S. Army: 17 top; IST Sports: 2 left; iStockphoto/filo: 17 left helicopter; SEAL + SWCC Scout Team: back cover, 3 bottom, 12 bottom, 16 humvee, 20, 24 top; Shutterstock, Inc./Mushakesa: 26 t-shirt template and throughout; U.S. Navy: 4 (Mass Communication Specialist 1st Class Dustin Kelling), 14 top (Mass Communication Specialist 2nd Class Erika N. Manzano), 8 bottom (Mass Communication Specialist 2nd Class John Scorza), 24 bottom (Mass Communication Specialist 2nd Class Matt Daniels), 10 bottom (Mass Communication Specialist 3rd Class Blake Midnight), 6 (Mass Communication Specialist 3rd Class Kristopher Kirsop), 24 center (Petty Officer 1st Class Shannon Renfroe), 22 (Petty Officer 2nd Class George R. Kusner), 12 top (Petty Officer 2nd Class William Parker), 1 SEAL logo and throughout, 28 Navy logo; U.S. Army: 15 bottom (1st Sgt Brandon McGuire, 1-28IN, 4IBCT), 11 top (John D. Helms), 13 background (Patrick A. Albright), 9 (Patrick Albright/MCoE PAO), 25 center (Pfc. Gabriel Segura), 25 top (Sgt. Richard W. Jones Jr.), 5 (Spc. Steven Hitchcock, 55th Signal Company (Combat Camera), 15 top (Sue Ulibarri), 7 (U.S. Army photo by Spc. Steven Hitchcock), 13 inset; Vector-Images.com: 1 Ranger tab and throughout, 19 Ranger scroll and throughout, 19 Ranger insignia and throughout.

Illustrations on pages 30 and 31 by David Biedrzycki.

Thank you to my favorite SEALs, Bill Garnett, Rudy Boesch, and Wyman Howard, and my favorite Rangers, too numerous to mention.

— J.P.

ISBN 978-0-545-83700-2

10 9 8 7 6 5 4 3 2 1          16 17 18 19 20

Printed in the U.S.A.

First printing 2016

Who do you think is tougher?

A US Navy SEAL or a US Army Ranger? This is not a fight! They are on the same team: the United States of America.

This book explains what each warrior does so well.

# US NAVY

**DEFINITION**
SEAL stands for
**SE**a, **A**ir, **L**and.

**NAVY FACT**
A man or woman
in the Navy is
called a sailor.

The US Navy is a fighting and protection armed force
consisting of ships, boats, submarines, aircraft, and sailors.

SEALs are an elite quick-attack force.
They are manned, trained, and equipped by the US Navy.

# US ARMY

The US Army is a fighting force of soldiers.

The Rangers are an elite quick-strike force. They are
manned, trained, and equipped by the US Army.

# SEAL HISTORY

The SEALs were established by President John F. Kennedy in 1962 as a small, elite maritime military force to conduct unconventional warfare. They carry out the small-unit, secret missions that large forces with ships, tanks, jets, or submarines can't.

In World War II, these elite combatants were often called frogmen. They cleared beaches in the Pacific and in Normandy, before D-Day. They later had operations in Vietnam, Panama, Kosovo, Iraq, Afghanistan, and more.

**NAME FACT**
SEALs used to be called UDT (Underwater Demolition Teams).

**FROGMAN FACT**
Before UDT, they were called NCDU (Naval Combat Demolition Units).

# RANGER HISTORY

Modern Army Ranger history begins in 1974, when the Army determined the need for permanent battalions of elite, quick, light, highly skilled infantry soldiers. The existing six battalions were combined in 1986 into the 75th Ranger Regiment.

But there were Rangers long before 1974. Various Ranger units fought in the Revolutionary War, the War of 1812, and the Civil War. Some seventy-five years later, during World War II, Ranger units reappeared. Rangers fought again in the Korean War, the Vietnam War, and other conflicts.

# BUD/S

## BASIC UNDERWATER DEMOLITION / SEAL

Are you tough enough to become a SEAL? Sailors start out in BUD/S (Basic Underwater Demolition/SEAL).

**Phase One / Green Helmets:** Candidates compete in eight weeks of teamwork with physical, mental, and water challenges.

You need an excellent time in a four-mile beach run and a two-mile ocean swim. Many sailors wonder if this was a good idea!

**DID YOU KNOW?**
Passing each phase earns a candidate the right to wear different-colored helmets.

8

# AIRBORNE

All Ranger candidates must complete Airborne School, where they learn how to static-line parachute. They do not free-fall jump. Then they move on to RASP.

**DEFINITION**
A *ripcord* is the cord that is pulled to open a parachute.

**PARACHUTE FACT**
In static-line parachuting, the soldier does not pull his own ripcord. Free-fall jumpers pull their own ripcords.

# BUD/S
## BASIC UNDERWATER DEMOLITION / SEAL

**Phase Two / Blue Helmets:** Candidates undergo eight weeks of underwater combat training. They try to survive in freezing-cold water, tricky currents, and huge waves. Candidates can quit at any time.

**Phase Three / Red Helmets:** Candidates spend nine weeks learning weapons, demolitions, navigation, patrolling, rappelling, and small-unit tactics.

Even if you pass BUD/S, you're not a SEAL yet!

# RASP

## RANGER ASSESSMENT AND SELECTION PROGRAM

RASP is eight weeks of intense physical, mental, and military training. Soldiers compete to get placed in a Ranger battalion and hope to get a slot at Ranger School.

**RECENT FACT**
RASP used to be called RIP (Ranger Indoctrination Program).

Many of the soldiers drop out within the first two weeks and return to a regular infantry unit. RASP could be summed up as: "Are you tough enough?"

You have graduated from RASP. You have earned your tan beret. Report to a Ranger battalion!

# SQT
## SEAL QUALIFICATION TRAINING

Candidates who get through BUD/S move on to eight weeks of SQT. Here they learn to be marksmen using different types of weapons.

They learn to use an underwater rebreather and other water-survival skills.

SEALs also learn teamwork and trust in small four-man fire teams.

# RANGER SCHOOL
## RAP WEEK

After a soldier is accepted into Ranger School, the first week is called Ranger Assessment Phase (RAP). RAP week is a tough physical and mental challenge.

**QUALIFICATION FACT**
More than one-third of candidates fail to meet the Ranger standard during RAP week and are dropped from the course.

# SQT
## SEAL QUALIFICATION TRAINING

Candidates also learn cold-weather skills, land navigation, and parachuting.

**HALO VS. HAHO**
Another way to parachute is HALO (High Altitude Low Opening). HAHO is High Altitude High Opening.

# RANGER SCHOOL

## DARBY PHASE
### NICKNAME: CRAWL

> **DEFINITION**
> A *ruck march* is a hike with full gear.

> **WORLD WAR II FACT**
> Darby is named after William O. Darby, the first Ranger commander.

In squad-size units, soldiers learn to plan, patrol, and execute missions while under mental and physical stress.

## MOUNTAIN PHASE
### NICKNAME: WALK

Food- and sleep-deprived candidates lead platoons through patrolling operations in rugged mountains.

SEAL candidates also learn medical skills so they can care for one another in battle. They learn explosives and demolitions.

All SEALs go through SERE training. It is a three-week, highly secretive course. SERE stands for:

# SERE

- Survival
- Evasion
- Resistance
- Escape

TOP SECRET

SERE training stresses the US military code of conduct, survival skills, evading capture, and how to behave as a prisoner of war.

zīmogs

tiiviste

# LANGUAGE

σφραγίδα

печать

密封

SEALs attend two months of language school. Knowing how to speak a local language helps any operation.

vulë    dichtung

ابی کوخ

# RANGER SCHOOL
## SWAMP PHASE
### NICKNAME: RUN

Soldiers learn water crossings, small boat movements, and swamp operations while learning to patrol in harsh conditions.

**DROPOUT FACT**
Less than half of the candidates who start the course will graduate.

# OTHER COMPARISONS

Some Rangers go to SERE, or language school, but it is not a requirement.

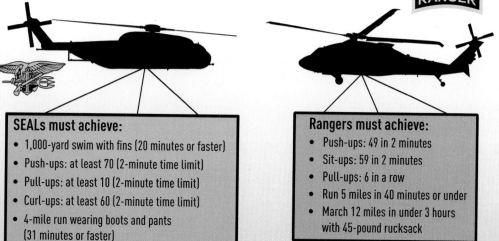

RANGER

**SEALs must achieve:**
- 1,000-yard swim with fins (20 minutes or faster)
- Push-ups: at least 70 (2-minute time limit)
- Pull-ups: at least 10 (2-minute time limit)
- Curl-ups: at least 60 (2-minute time limit)
- 4-mile run wearing boots and pants (31 minutes or faster)

**Rangers must achieve:**
- Push-ups: 49 in 2 minutes
- Sit-ups: 59 in 2 minutes
- Pull-ups: 6 in a row
- Run 5 miles in 40 minutes or under
- March 12 miles in under 3 hours with 45-pound rucksack

The standards may look easy on paper, but the cadre mentally challenge you while grading.

After SQT, you've earned your trident. Congratulations! You are now a SEAL. Report to a SEAL team!

# TRIDENT

The anchor symbolizes the US Navy.

The eagle symbolizes the SEALs' ability to quickly attack from the air.

The trident symbolizes Neptune.

The pistol symbolizes that SEALs also work on land. The pistol is cocked and ready to fire, for SEALs are ready at all times.

**SEA FACT**
The ocean is the toughest environment for a warrior.

**ROMAN GOD FACT**
Neptune was the Roman god of the sea. SEALs have a connection to the sea.

# TAB

A soldier earns a Ranger tab after completing Ranger School. A tab is an insignia, or badge, worn on a uniform. Every Army unit has its own special insignia.

# SCROLL

Only Rangers serving in the elite 75th Ranger Regiment may wear this insignia.

# DISTINCTIVE UNIT INSIGNIA

The star represents Burma. The sun represents China. These are two countries in which the Rangers fought in World War II.

The lightning bolt signifies the Rangers' quick-strike capabilities.

# SEAL EQUIPMENT

rebreather
equipment

wet suit

M4A1
carbine

fins

**Navy SEAL Survival Kit**
includes: map, fire-starting
kit, flares, wire, signal mirror,
compass, mini multi-tool,
LED squeeze light, Kevlar
(bulletproof) vests, helmet,
safety pins, and more.

# RANGER EQUIPMENT

**night-vision goggles**

**helmet** with:
helmet light
wind/dust goggles
visible/infrared
strobe light

**M4A1 carbine** with:
4X scope
day/night laser
tactical light

**radio**

**INFRARED FACT**
Infrared strobe light
guides aircraft to
our soldiers.

**DEFINITION**
A *flash bang* is a
grenade that sounds
like gunfire to
confuse the enemy.

**safety
lanyard**

**Ranger Kit** includes: body
armor, grenades, flash bangs,
ammo, water source, first aid,
tourniquet, radio, flex-cuffs,
batteries, snacks, C4 explosives,
and more.

**DEFINITION**
*Flex-cuffs* are plastic
handcuffs.

# NIGHT VISION

Night-vision goggles allow you to see when it's pitch-black out. What you see will look like this.

All Navy SEALs use night-vision goggles.

## INFRARED FACT

Night vision allows SEALs to see infrared light. Infrared light is light that can't be seen by the human eye.

## UNSELFISH FACT

All SEALs are volunteers. No one forces anyone to become an elite warrior.

# GOGGLES

All Rangers also carry night-vision goggles.

SEALs and Rangers often use many of the same pieces of equipment.

# HOW CAN SEALs GET TO BATTLE?

**SWIM** - They could swim or scuba dive to the site.

**PARACHUTE** - They could parachute in. SEALs practice static-line parachuting and free-fall parachuting.

**INFLATABLE BOATS** - Inflatable boats are light and fast. They are a proven way to get SEALs to their mission.

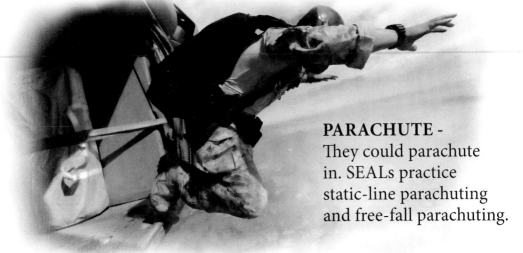

# WHAT IS THE QUICKEST WAY TO GET RANGERS TO THE FIGHT?

## GROUND INFILTRATION
Rangers often walk, jog, or run to battle.

## FAST-ROPE FROM HELICOPTER
Rangers fast-rope from Chinooks, Blackhawks, and Little Birds.
Ranger dogs fast-rope, too.

## PARACHUTE
The soldier in charge of a jump is called the jumpmaster.

## NOT THAT HIGH
Rangers usually jump from only about 1,000 feet in the air. This gets them to the ground as fast as possible.

25

# THANK YOU, SEALs

Our favorite SEAL T-shirts:

NAVY SEALs

THE ONLY EASY DAY
WAS YESTERDAY

READY TO LEAD
NEVER QUIT
READY TO FOLLOW

US NAVY SEALs

US NAVY
SEALs

WHEN SOMETHING
ABSOLUTELY
POSITIVELY
HAS TO BE DESTROYED
OVERNIGHT

# THANK YOU, RANGERS

Our favorite Ranger T-shirts:

MOST PEOPLE **KNOCK.** WE'RE NOT MOST PEOPLE!

**ARMY RANGERS**

RLTW

SUA SPONTE

RANGER

RANGER

75 RGT

**RANGERS**
LEAD THE WAY

# NAVAL
# SPECIAL WARFARE

Here are the locations of the SEAL teams.

**WEST COAST:**
San Diego, California,
is the home of SEAL
Teams 1, 3, 5, and 7.

Hawaii is the home
of SEAL Delivery
Vehicle Team 1.

**EAST COAST:**
Little Creek, Virginia,
is the home of SEAL
Teams 2, 4, 8, and 10.

SEAL Team 6 is secret.
"We are not talking about it."

# 75TH RANGER REGIMENT

Here are the locations of the Ranger battalions.

Fort Lewis, Washington, is the home of the 2nd Ranger Battalion.

**FAMOUS FACT**
Daniel Boone and Abraham Lincoln were Rangers.

**HEADQUARTERS FACT**
75th Regiment headquarters is located in Fort Benning, Georgia.

**GEOGRAPHY FACT**
Fort Benning, Georgia, is home to infantry basic training, advanced infantry training, Airborne school, and RASP.

Fort Benning, Georgia, is the home of the 3rd Ranger Battalion.

Special Troops Battalion (STB) is also located at Fort Benning.

Hunter Army Airfield, Georgia, is the home of the 1st Ranger Battalion.

Who is tougher? A SEAL or a Ranger? If we had a contest, who could hold his breath the longest underwater? The SEAL would win.

If we had a race between a SEAL and a Ranger up a steep mountain carrying fifty-pound rucksacks, protective plates, and rifles, who would win?

The Ranger.

If both went to a shooting range, and the SEAL and Ranger shot at stationary and moving targets using different weapons, who would be the best shot?

It's a tie; they are both excellent marksmen.

the SEAL and Ranger had to swim a mile
from a ship to a submarine in freezing
water with huge waves, the
SEAL would win.

During battle, if a SEAL and Ranger each had
to carry a wounded comrade to safety,
who would do it better?

This is also a tie,
because both warriors
are trained never to
leave anyone behind.

In a thick forest,
with little sleep, who
could find his way
through the hills
and valleys better?

The Ranger.

Who is tougher? A SEAL or a Ranger? They are both tough, physically and mentally. These highly trained warriors are on the same team. They serve America and protect our freedoms.

**FACT**
Only one out of about 100 sailors is tough and smart enough to qualify to be a SEAL.

**FACT**
Only one out of about 100 soldiers is tough and smart enough to qualify to be a Ranger.

**FACT**
Only one in 64,000 Americans becomes a SEAL or a Ranger.